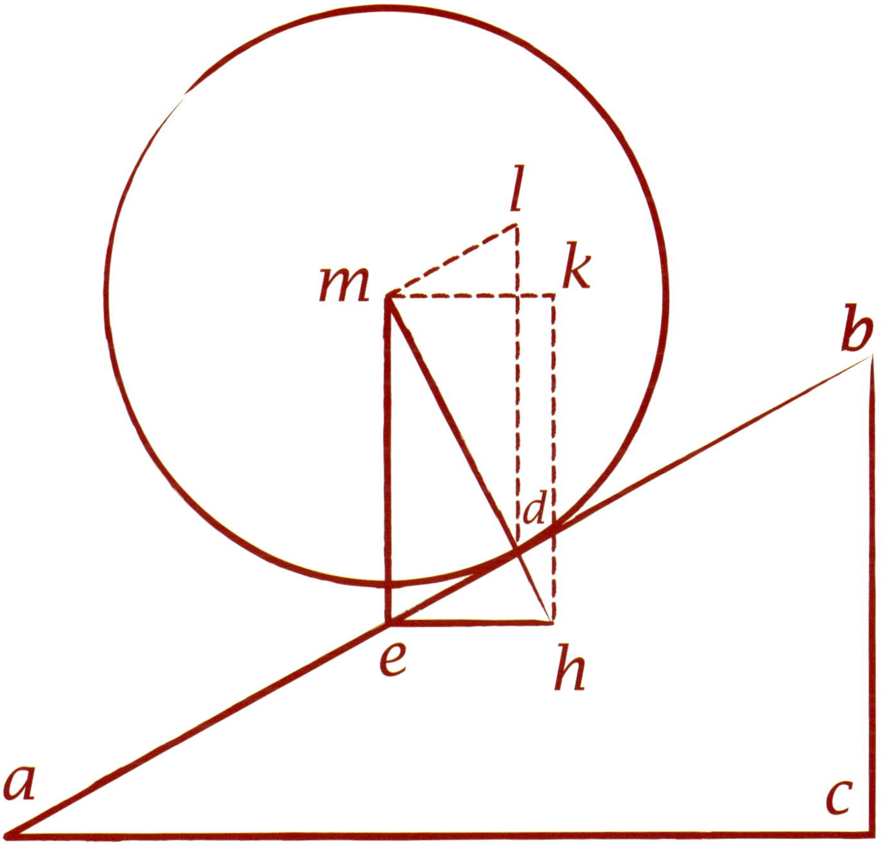

A Timeline of Mathematics and Computers

Counting Pebbles to Writing Code

WORLD BOOK

World Book
a Scott Fetzer company
Chicago

World Book, Inc.
180 North LaSalle Street
Suite 900
Chicago, Illinois 60601
USA

For information about other World Book publications, call 1-800-WORLDBK (967-5325).

For information about sales to schools and libraries, call 1-800-975-3250 (United States) or 1-800-837-5365 (Canada).

Produced for World Book, Inc. by Bailey Publishing Associates Ltd.

Library of Congress Cataloging-in-Publication Data

Title: Counting pebbles to writing code: a timeline of mathematics and computers.
Description: Chicago: World Book, Inc., a Scott Fetzer company, 2016. | Series: A timeline of ... | Includes index.
Identifiers: LCCN 2016012915 | ISBN 9780716635413
Subjects: LCSH: Mathematics--History--Juvenile literature. | Computers--History--Juvenile literature.
Classification: LCC QA141.3 .C68 2016 | DDC 510.9--dc23
LC record available at https://lccn.loc.gov/2016012915

Counting Pebbles to Writing Code: A Timeline of Mathematics and Computers ISBN: 978-0-7166-3541-3
A Timeline of... Set ISBN: 978-0-7166-3539-0
E-book ISBN: 978-0-7166-3550-5 (ePUB3 format)

Printed in China by Shenzhen Wing King Tong Paper Products Co., Ltd., Guangdong Province
1st printing July 2016

Acknowledgments

Cover photo: Shutterstock (Morphart Creation).

Bridgeman Picture Library 7 right (British Museum/De Agostini), 9 left (Vatican Museums and Galleries), 11 (Private Collection), 12 (Universal History Archive/UIG), 13 (Ancient Art and Architecture Collection), 14 (Private Collection), 16 (Terence Nunn), 17 (Universal History Archive/UIG), 18 (School of African and Oriental Studies), 19 right (De Agostini), 23 (CNAM, Conservatoire National des Arts et Metiers/Archives Charmet), 25 left (Private Collection), 25 right (Worshipful Company of Clockmakers' Collection).

CERN 35.

Corbis 4 top (G. Dagli Orti), 19 left (Bettmann), 20 (Bettmann), 26 left, 27 (Heritage Images), 28, 30 (Heritage Images), 31, 32 (Bettmann), 33 (K. Lemm/dpa), 35 (J. Brady/epa), 37 (Courtesy: Maryam Mirzakhan).

Getty 10 (Louisa Goulamaki/AFP Photo), 15 (Universal History Archive), 29 (Fred Stein Archive), 34 (Science & Society Picture Library).

Shutterstock 4 bottom (Fotografos), 7 left (P. Hermes Furian), 8 left (Tupungato), 22 (Everett Historical), 24 (Marzolino), 26 right (T. Jenner).

Wilhelm Krucken 21.

World Book 6, 8 right, 9 right.

Glossary There is a glossary of terms on page 38. Terms defined in the glossary are in type that **looks like this** (called *boldface type*) on their first appearance on any *spread* (two facing pages).

Circa Some dates are written with *c.* before the year. The *c.* stands for *circa.* Circa means *approximately.* For example, with c. 250 B.C., the phrase is read as "circa 250 B.C.," meaning *approximately 250 B.C.* Circa can be used with both B.C. and A.D. dates.

Contents

Counting Pebbles to Writing Code

A Timeline of Mathematics and Computers

Early people marked clay tablets to keep records that used *numerals* (symbols that stand for numbers). They also used pebbles, bones, and their fingers to count.

People write codes in numerals for all of the programs that run on a computer. The codes are stored on tiny computer chips, like the squares shown below.

Introduction

Mathematics Through the Ages

Mathematics is much older than written history. More than 20,000 years ago, people probably counted with their fingers and used pebbles to record numbers. They drew lines on bones and on cave walls to stand for numbers. Later, farmers and traders learned more complex mathematics to keep records.

As society developed, mathematics and science became more closely connected. People used mathematics to create amazing inventions. Some of these inventions, in turn, helped people use mathematics. In the early days of the computer, the device was mainly used to speed up *calculations* (mathematics problems). Today, people use computers in countless ways. But at their cores, computers are mathematical machines.

There are many *branches* (different kinds) of mathematics that are used every day:

- *Arithmetic* is about numbers—whole numbers (0, 1, 2, 3, and so on), fractions (such as ½ and ¼), and decimals (0.5 and 0.25, for example). Arithmetic is used to add, subtract, multiply, and divide.
- **Algebra** uses letters, such as x and y, to stand for unknown quantities. With algebra, people can solve more complex mathematics problems.
- **Geometry** is the study of shapes. *Plane geometry* uses squares, circles, triangles, and other flat shapes. *Solid geometry* uses shapes that take up space, including cubes and spheres.
- **Trigonometry** involves the sides and angles of triangles.
- **Calculus** is the study of changing quantities.
- **Probability** uses numbers to find out how likely an event is to happen or not.
- **Set theory** involves groups of numbers, objects, or ideas.

To learn more, follow the timeline through this book to trace the history of mathematic discoveries and computer inventions from the earliest civilizations to the present day.

Chapter 1

Ancient World Mathematics

Before 20,000 B.C.—c. 200 B.C.

Prehistoric people probably counted using their fingers. They counted how many animals were in a herd. They kept track of the days between full moons. To record numbers, they could set out pebbles. They also could tie knots in a cord or cut marks into bone, stone, or wood.

By about 3000 B.C., people in ancient Egypt were using a picture writing system called *hieroglyphics*. They used certain hieroglyphs to stand for numbers. A written

Before 20,000 B.C.

Prehistoric people in central Africa cut notches into bones for counting.

c. 3000 B.C.

Ancient Egyptians used a hieroglyph numeral system. They used symbols to stand for groups of 10, 100, 1,000, 10,000, and 100,000.

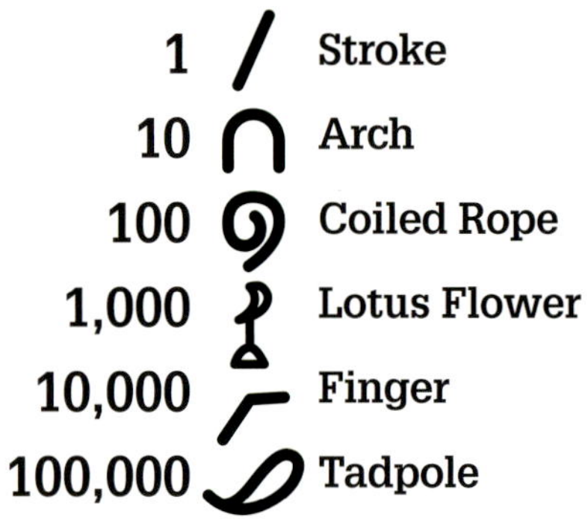

They wrote numbers by putting these symbols next to one another. For example, they wrote the number 1,326 like this:

c. 2500 B.C.

Traders in the Indus Valley civilization, in what is now India and Pakistan, used standard weights and measures as counting tools.

c. 2100 B.C.

The Mesopotamians used a cuneiform numeral system. They did not count in groups of 10, like the Egyptians. Instead, they counted in groups of 60. We still count in groups of 60 today to tell time. There are 60 seconds in a minute and 60 minutes in an hour.

symbol that stands for a number is called a **numeral.** Today, we use the numerals 0, 1, 2, 3, 4, and so on. The Egyptians' numeral system was simpler than ours. But even a simple numeral system helped the Egyptians become a great civilization.

East of Egypt, people in Mesopotamia (in what is now Iraq) used numerals to count. Mesopotamians did not write with hieroglyphs. Instead, they made wedge-shaped marks in wet clay tablets. The tablet was then dried in the sun to preserve the writing upon it. This writing system is called *cuneiform (kyoo NEE uh fawrm).*

Both the Egyptians and Mesopotamians developed systems of mathematics. They used mathematics to measure fields, count goods for trade, and build huge stone and brick pyramids. They also used mathematics to study the stars.

2000 B.C.

The Egyptians also created a "magic 3-4-5 triangle." They stretched a long rope around three stakes in the ground. The stakes were placed so that the triangle's sides measured 3, 4, and 5 units long. They knew that such a triangle always has one **square angle.** Square angles proved useful for measuring fields and building pyramids.

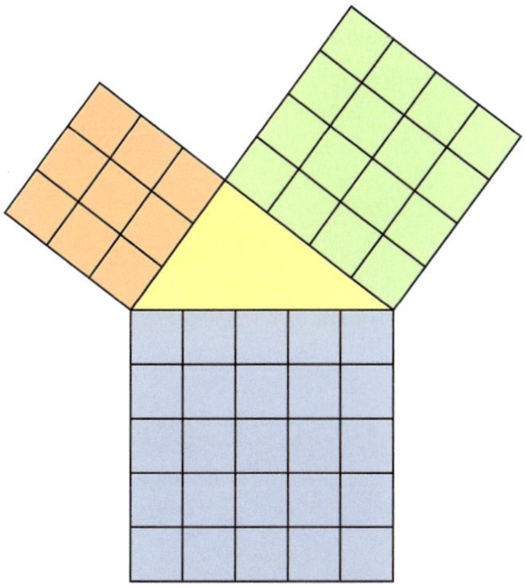

1650 B.C.

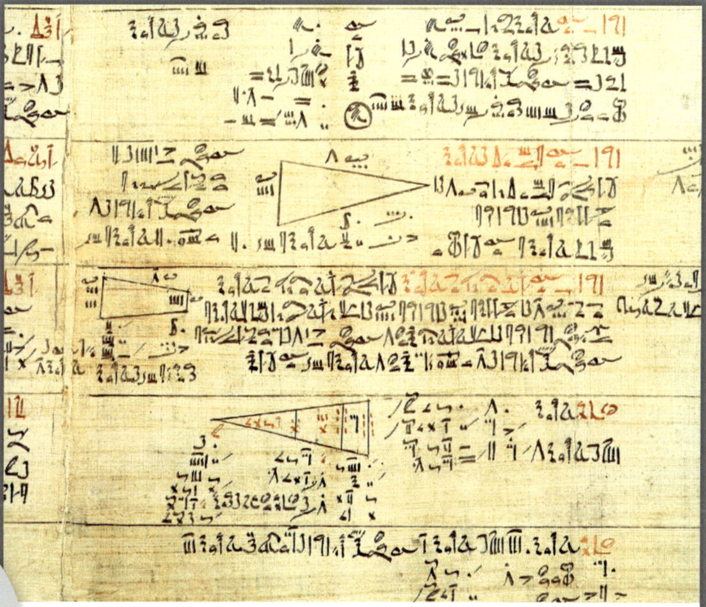

An Egyptian scroll, later named the *Rhind Mathematical Papyrus*, copied by a scribe named Ahmes, shows an early example of **algebra.**

1400's B.C.

The Phoenicians invented an alphabet. The new writing system spread to such people as the ancient Greeks and Romans, who later used alphabet letters as numbers.

Ancient World Mathematics

Before 20,000 B.C.—c. 200 B.C.

Across the Mediterranean Sea from Egypt, people in another large civilization became masters of mathematics. Philosophers, or thinkers, of ancient Greece were fascinated by the shapes in **geometry.** The word *geometry* comes from the Greek words for *Earth* and *to measure.* Philosophers proved many new facts about shapes and numbers. They used **logic**—step-by-step thinking—to show how new facts followed from older ones.

For example, the ancient Egyptians discovered that a "3-4-5" triangle has one **square angle.** Later, the Babylonians, who also lived in Mesopotamia, studied the

Thales, a Greek philosopher, is thought to have lived from around 625 B.C. to 546 B.C. According to tradition, Thales was the first to prove a geometric idea with step-by-step logic.

c. 625 B.C.

c. 580 B.C.

Greek philosopher Pythagoras is thought to have been born around 580 B.C. He taught geometry and explored numbers. His death date is unknown.

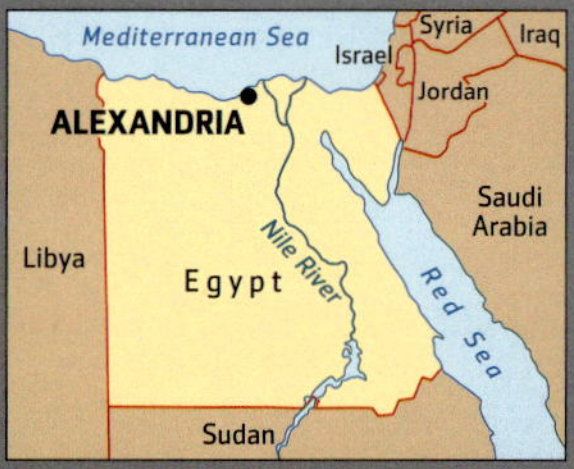

Alexander the Great (356 B.C.-323 B.C.) founded the city of Alexandria in Egypt. The city became a great center of learning.

331 B.C.

"3-4-5" triangle. They discovered another interesting pattern about this triangle. If the triangle's sides are turned into squares, then the "3" and "4" squares, added together, have the same area, or surface space, as the "5" square. Using the work of the Egyptians and Babylonians, Greek philosophers used logic to prove that this fact is true for any triangle with a square angle. Their proof became known as the *Pythagorean theorem*. It is named after the philosopher Pythagoras.

The Greeks also used facts about triangles and angles to prove other ideas true. One Greek philosopher, Eratosthenes (276? B.C.-195? B.C.), used geometry to measure the size of Earth. He did this without leaving his home in northern Africa. He studied the angles of shadows and used logic to learn more about Earth.

Ancient Greek mathematician Euclid is thought to have lived from around 330 B.C. to 270 B.C. Euclid wrote a geometry book called *Elements*. This book gathered all of the Greeks' knowledge about geometry into one place. Euclid also explored **prime numbers.** A prime number can be divided evenly only by 1 and itself. Euclid proved there must be an unlimited amount of prime numbers.

c. 330 B.C.

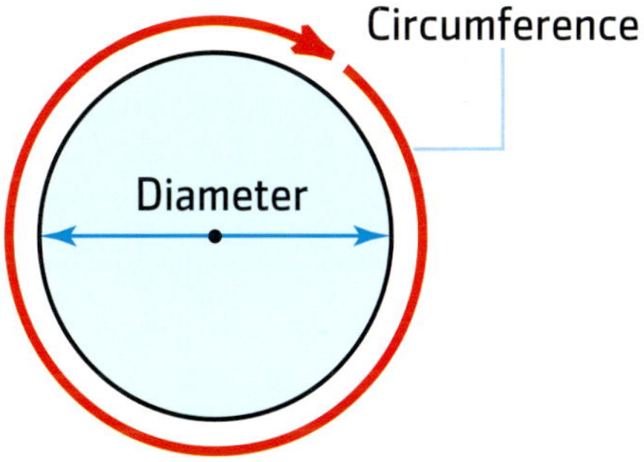

Ancient Greek mathematician Archimedes is thought to have lived from around 287 B.C. to 212 B.C. He explored one of the most important numbers in mathematics—**pi.** Pi—sometimes written with the Greek letter π—has to do with circles. A circle's *circumference* (outer boundary line) divided by its *diameter* (line that crosses through the center) always equals pi. Pi is not exactly equal to any number.

c. 287 B.C.

Chapter 2

Mathematics Goes to Work

c. 100 B.C.—Late A.D. 400's

Ancient Greek civilization and ideas spread to such places as Egypt, Rome, and a region now known as the Middle East. The ancient Romans eventually conquered ancient Greece. The Romans founded a huge empire. Unlike the Greeks, the Romans were less interested in studying mathematics for its own sake. Instead, the Romans wanted to put mathematics to work.

Roman *engineers* (people who use mathematics and science to plan and build

In 1900, explorers found a bronze, clocklike device underwater in a sunken ship off the Greek island of Antikythera. Known as the Antikythera mechanism, it was once used to predict the movements of the sun and planets. Built around 100 B.C., it is the earliest known computing device.

c. 100 B.C.

c. 100's B.C.

The Chinese founded a large empire in Asia. They developed many important mathematical ideas. The Chinese used *negative numbers*—values less than zero. They used a device called an *abacus* to help solve problems. An abacus had columns of beads strung on several counting rods. Other peoples also used this device. One early Chinese mathematics book was called *Nine Chapters on the Mathematical Art*. It was a handbook of useful mathematics problems.

structures) used mathematics for many purposes. They built useful roadways across their empire. To supply cities with fresh water, engineers built aqueducts. These gently angled waterways carried water from high mountain springs to the cities. The Romans also constructed huge domed buildings. They needed to use **geometry** when building—otherwise, the domes would collapse!

The Romans used letters to stand for numbers. There were seven basic letter symbols: I (1), V (5), X (10), L (50), C (100), D (500), and M (1,000). To write the number 3,762, a Roman wrote MMMDCCLXII. MMM (3,000), then DCC (500 + 200), then LX (50 + 10), and finally, II (2). The Roman numeral system was complex. But people in Europe used these numerals every day for hundreds of years. You can still see Roman numerals carved into old buildings and on many clock faces.

46 B.C.

Roman leader Julius Caesar (100 B.C.-44 B.C.)ordered the creation of a new calendar. An astronomer named Sosigenes made the new calendar with one year made up of 12 months. Each month had 30 or 31 days, except for February. Named after Caesar, the Julian calendar was widely used for more than 1,500 years.

A.D. 150

Greek astronomer Ptolemy (A.D. 100?-A.D. 165?) studied the planets while living in Alexandria, Egypt. He wrote a book entitled *Mathematical Composition.* This work was so admired that it became known as the *Almagest,* meaning the *greatest.* He wrote that Earth was the center of the universe, a belief shared by many people until the 1500's.

Mathematics Goes to Work

c. 100 B.C.—Late A.D. 400's

In China and India, people had little contact with the ancient Egyptians, Mesopotamians, Greeks, and Romans. But the Chinese and Indians developed many of the same mathematical ideas as these other peoples. For example, Chinese mathematicians invented versions of the Pythagorean theorem. They also narrowed down the value of **pi.**

In India, mathematicians used symbols for 1, 2, 3, 4, 5, 6, 7, 8, and 9. They developed an important idea called *place value.* When we write the number 125, what we mean is "1 hundred, 2 tens, and 5 ones." The values of the 1, 2, and 5

By A.D. 250, the Maya were using a symbol for zero. The Mayan counting system was based on groups of 20, instead of 10 or 60. A dot represented the number 1 and a bar represented 5. They had special symbols for 0. Mayan priests used both mathematics and *astronomy* (the study of all of space) to create accurate yearly calendars, such as the part of one calendar shown below.

A.D. 250

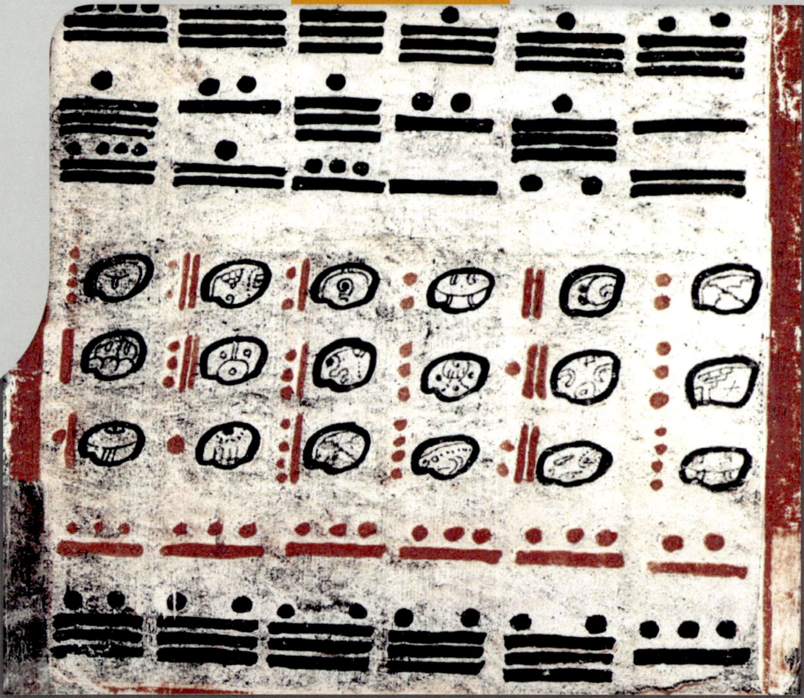

A.D. 263

Chinese mathematician Liu Hui (A.D. 255-A.D. 295) studied the Gou-Gu theorem. This theorem, or rule, explains the relationship between the three sides of a square-angle triangle. The Gou-Gu theorem is also known as the Pythagorean theorem. Hui also accurately calculated pi. To find the value of pi, he made a figure with 3,072 equal sides to create a circlelike shape.

depend on their *place* in the number. Writing numbers this way saves much time. Place value also makes it easier to calculate arithmetic.

For place value to work well, the Indians needed a symbol to represent nothing. This symbol is the number zero (0). The Babylonians used such a symbol. But they didn't use it with place value. In fact, the Maya, who lived in what is now Central America and Mexico, developed their own similar mathematics systems. They were the first people to use a zero in place value. But, the Maya lived so far away from Indian and Chinese peoples that their ideas never spread to Asia or Europe. The Indians eventually came up with their own way of writing "nothing"—0, the symbol we use today.

Hypatia (A.D. 370?-A.D. 415) was the first known woman mathematician. She wrote commentary, or notes, on mathematics texts and gave public lectures on science and philosophy. She died during riots in the city of Alexandria in Egypt.

A.D. 415

A.D. 476

Indian astronomer Aryabhata is thought to have lived from around A.D. 476 to A.D. 550. He wrote an important book on mathematics and astronomy called the *Aryabhatiya.* It contained some of the earliest examples of **algebra** problems.

Chapter 3

Studying Mathematics

A.D. 500—Mid-1300's

The fall of the Western Roman Empire during the late A.D. 400's marks the beginning of the **Middle Ages** in Europe. Much ancient knowledge was lost in western Europe at this time. The Eastern Roman Empire became known as the Byzantine Empire. In the Byzantine Empire, ancient Greek and Roman texts were preserved and mathematical study continued to develop. Byzantine engineers used advanced mathematics to construct huge domed buildings. One important domed structure is the Hagia Sophia, a two-story cathedral located in what is now

A.D. 628

Brahmagupta (A.D. 598-A.D. 665), an Indian scientist, wrote a mathematics text that included rules for zero. He proposed that a number multiplied by zero becomes zero. We still use this rule today.

A.D. 700's

Englishman Alcuin of York (A.D. 735-A.D. 804) wrote one of the first mathematics textbooks in Europe. He called the book *Problems to Sharpen the Young.*

c. A.D. 800

By A.D. 800, mathematicians in India had a decimal system that included zero. This advancement shaped the modern **numeral** system used today.

Istanbul, Turkey. The completion of the central dome showed that mathematics was useful to many people and jobs in society.

In the A.D. 600's, a new religion called *Islam* spread across the Middle East. In the lands of the Islamic Empire, scholars translated ancient texts into Arabic. Rulers of the Islamic Empire founded great libraries to help knowledge flow among people in Persia, India, and China. By the A.D. 800's, the Islamic capital of Baghdad (in what is now Iraq) was a center of learning that rivaled Alexandria, Egypt.

Scholars in the Baghdad region made advances in astronomy, medicine, and mathematics. Intellectuals from many lands came to study in Baghdad's library, named the House of Wisdom, to research and exchange ideas.

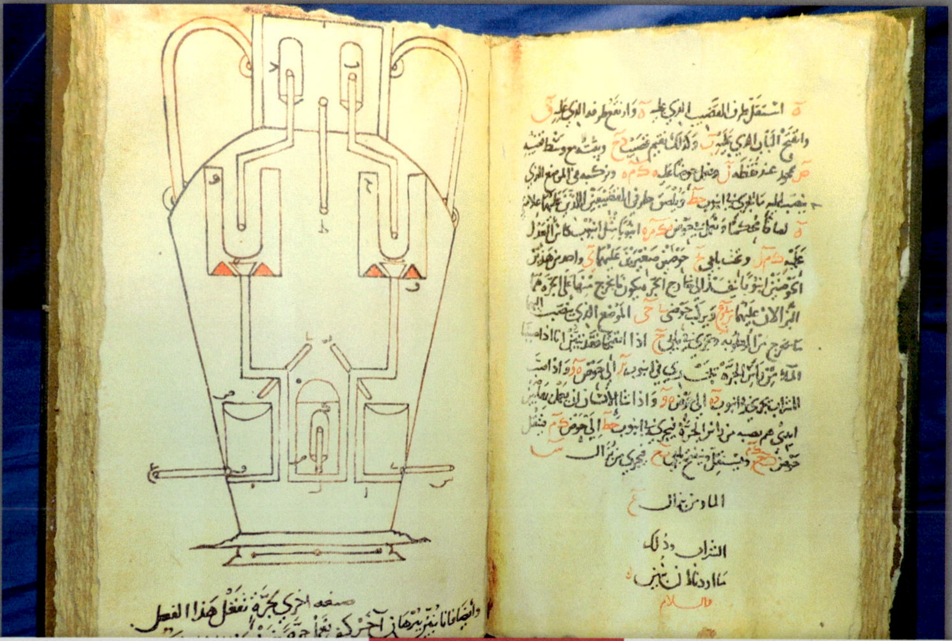

c. A.D. 850

Leader al-Ma'mun (A.D. 786-A.D. 833) founded a library and research center in Baghdad called the House of Wisdom. Here, scholars translated ancient Greek, Roman, and Indian works about mathematics and astronomy into Arabic. By the late A.D. 800's, the House of Wisdom held the biggest collection of texts in the world at the time. The *Book of Ingenious Devices* is a famous engineering text published by the Banu Musa brothers, who lived in the A.D. 800's and worked at the House of Wisdom.

Studying Mathematics

A.D. 500—Mid-1300's

Persian mathematician al-Khwarizmi introduced the idea of zero to the Islamic world. Al-Khwarizmi also wrote a book about **algebra.** The English word algebra comes from the Arabic word *al-jabr*, meaning *restoration* or *completion.* In algebra, such letters as *x* or *y* represent unknown numbers in an **equation.** An example of an algebra equation is x + 7 = 10. For this equation to be true, x must equal 3. Algebra is useful for solving everyday problems and became a widely studied branch of mathematics. Students still study algebra in schools around the world today.

A.D. 800's

Persian mathematician al-Khwarizmi (A.D. 780-A.D. 850) wrote about algebra. He helped to explain the number zero (0) to the Islamic Empire. The English word *zero* probably came from *ziphirum*, a Latin form of the Arabic word *sifr*. The Arabic word, in turn, comes from the Indian Sanskrit word *sunya*, meaning "empty." The idea of zero spread from the Islamic Empire and reached Europe by the late 1400's.

A.D. 800's

Arab scholar Abu Yusuf al-Kindi (died c. A.D. 870) wrote about Euclid's geometry and cryptography.

Abu Yusuf al-Kindi was another important scholar. Born in what is now Iraq during the A.D. 800's, al-Kindi wrote about **geometry,** philosophy, *optics* (the science of light and vision), and music. He was interested in **cryptography** using codes and ciphers. Al-Kindi proposed the idea of "frequency analysis." This codebreaking technique helps a person discover what a coded message means by studying how often certain letters appear in that message. Today, similar techniques are used to break into encrypted, or coded, computer files.

New mathematical ideas also spread to Europe, where monks in Christian monasteries had preserved some ancient Greek and Roman texts. Europeans learned about the "Arabic" or "Hindu-Arabic" **numeral** system by reading translations of Arabic texts. We still use Hindu-Arabic numerals (1, 2, 3,...) today.

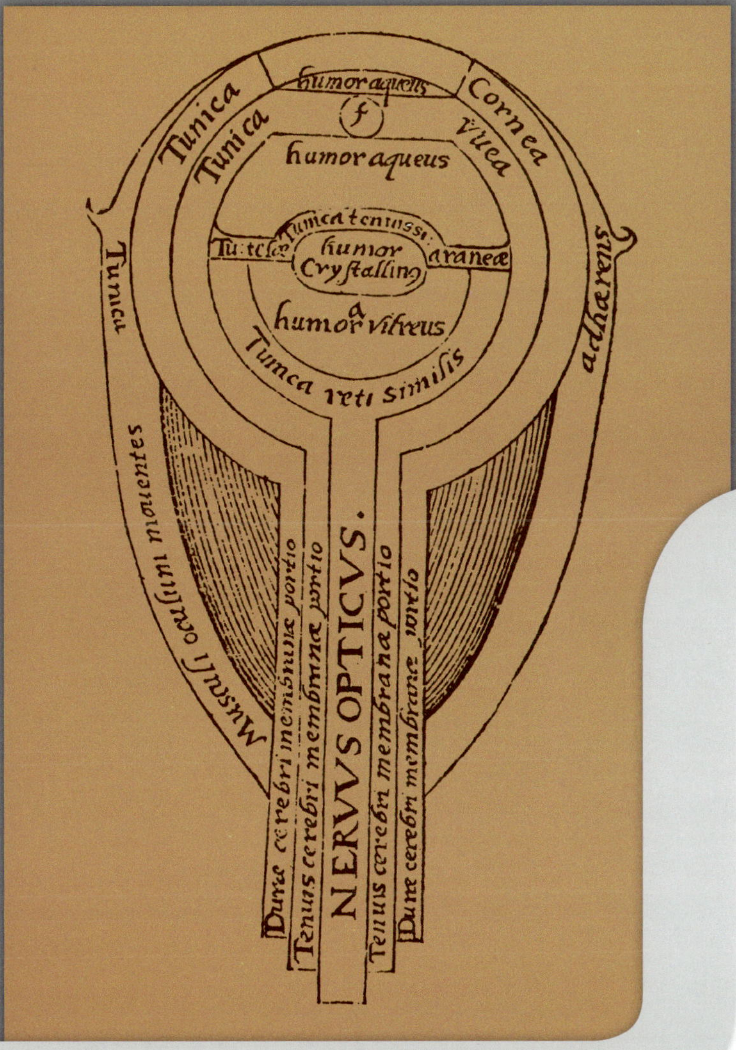

A.D. 965

Scientist and mathematician Ibn al-Haytham (A.D. 965-1040) was born in what is now Iraq. He studied geometry, **number theory,** and the angles of light rays entering the human eye. By showing how these light rays form images, he helped explain the mystery of vision. He is also called Alhazen in Latin.

Studying Mathematics

A.D. 500—Mid-1300's

By the **Middle Ages,** more Europeans were using mathematics for business. Due to war, trade, and education, more contact was made between peoples in Europe, Asia, and the Middle East. International traders used money to buy and sell goods. They needed advanced mathematical methods to record their sales. To meet this need, early banking systems developed in Italy in the 1200's. For more complex business, European traders and bankers needed to calculate accurately. Advanced mathematics allowed for more accurate ways to measure and weigh money.

People also wanted to use precise methods to count the passage of time

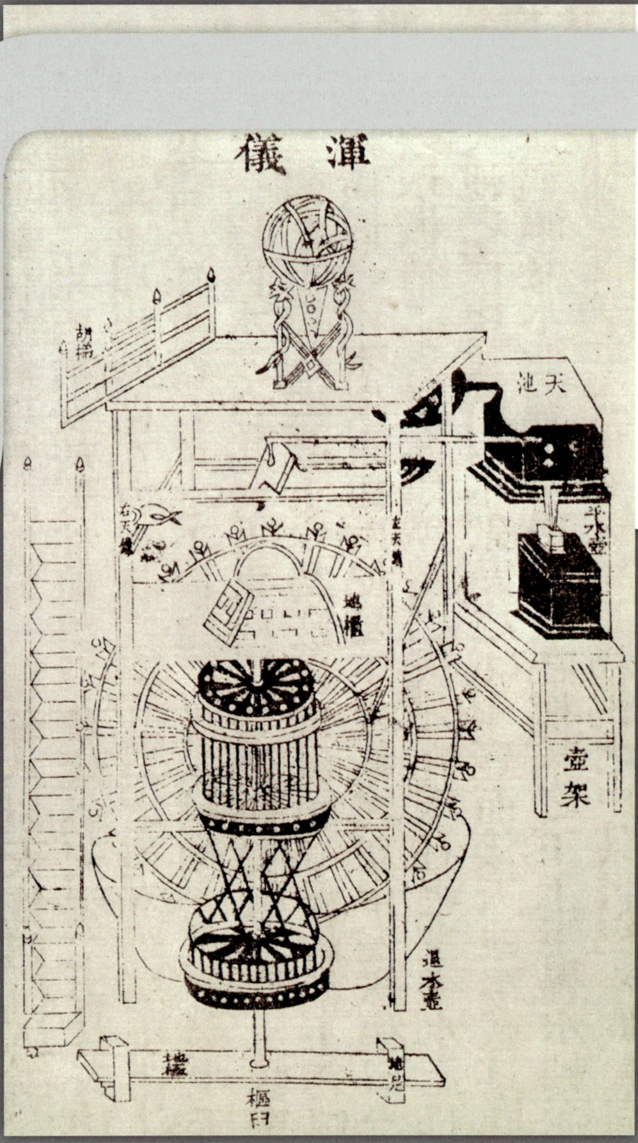

1092

Chinese astronomer and inventor Su-Sung (1020-1100) completed his huge, water-driven mechanical clock tower. The tower powered a large display of the planets and told the time.

1202

In his *Book of Calculation*, Italian mathematician Leonardo of Pisa, later known as Fibonacci (1170?-?), wrote about a special number sequence, or series. Every number in his sequence is the sum of the two numbers before it: 1, 1, 2, 3, 5, 8, 13... (2 = 1+1; 3 = 2+1; 5 = 3 +2; and so on). This sequence is known as the *Fibonacci sequence*. It is used in many branches of mathematics today.

throughout the day. In ancient times, people measured time with sundials (which mark the sun's position in the sky with a shadow) and by burning candles that were marked with hours of the day. In the late 1000's, Chinese inventor Su-Sung built a mechanical water-clock. The power from the water helped the clock count time automatically. In the 1200's, a new type of clock was made in Europe. These clocks were complex machines. Heavy weights were attached to huge wheels. As the weights moved, the wheels spun at a steady speed to count the time that passed.

Until the 1200's most Europeans still used Roman numerals when counting. Around 1192, Italian mathematician Leonardo of Pisa traveled to Muslim-ruled Algeria. There, he learned Arabic and many mathematical ideas. In 1202, he wrote his *Book of Calculation*. It explained the Hindu-Arabic numeral system and **algebra.**

1270's

English scientist Roger Bacon (1214-1294) wrote many works on mathematics, physics, and astronomy. He believed that people in Europe should adopt Hindu-Arabic numerals (1, 2, 3, 4...) instead of continuing to use Roman numerals.

Mechanical clocks were developed in Europe in the late 1200's. These early clocks had no hour hands or dial. They told time by ringing a bell.

Late 1200's

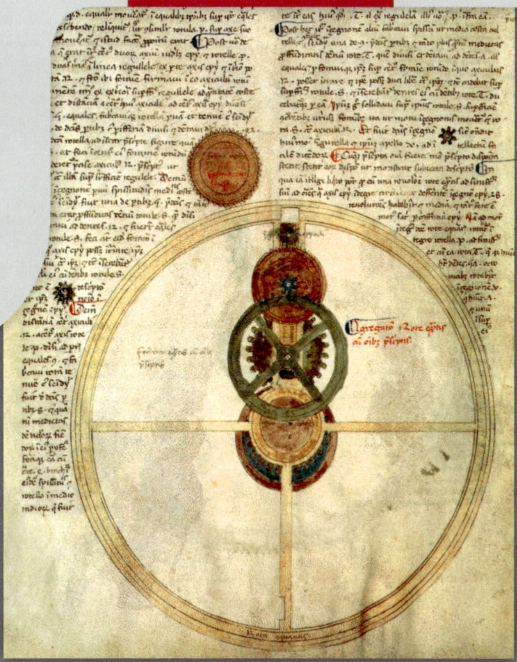

Mid-1300's

Clocks had a dial and hour hands to tell time.

Chapter 4

Renaissance Mathematics

Early 1400's—Late 1500's

The **Renaissance** was a period in European history from about 1300 to the 1600's when the study of mathematics and other sciences, art, literature, and history gained new importance. By the 1300's, Europeans had rediscovered much ancient mathematical knowledge. In the late 1400's, German inventor Johannes Gutenberg (1395?-1468?) created a printing press. Printing books with a machine was much faster than copying book pages by hand. With the printing press, new knowledge, including mathematics, spread far more quickly across the world.

1410

Filippo Brunelleschi (1377?-1446), an Italian architect, used mathematical concepts to create the first perspective paintings of a city. This artistic method gives a flat picture the feel of depth and distance.

1489

The first printed book with the plus (+) and minus (–) signs was published in Germany.

1533

In a book published after his death, a German mathematician known as Regiomontanus (1436-1476) established **trigonometry** as a separate branch of mathematics.

1543

In his book *On the Revolution of Heavenly Spheres*, Copernicus (1473-1543) stated that Earth revolved around the sun. This concept is known as *Copernican theory.*

During this time, European explorers sailed across the oceans. They did not have useful maps to guide their trips. Instead, explorers navigated the sea by looking at the angles of the sun, moon, and stars. This method was difficult and often led to serious navigational errors. Many explorers did not arrive where they intended or got lost at sea and never returned home.

With advanced mathematics, mapmakers were able to create better maps of the world. With more accurate maps, ocean exploration became safer. Mathematics also helped in the study of the planets. In 1543, two months after his death, a book by Polish astronomer Nicolaus Copernicus was published that stated Earth was not the center of the universe. He used mathematics to try to prove that the planets move around the sun. Few believed him, but mathematics eventually proved him correct.

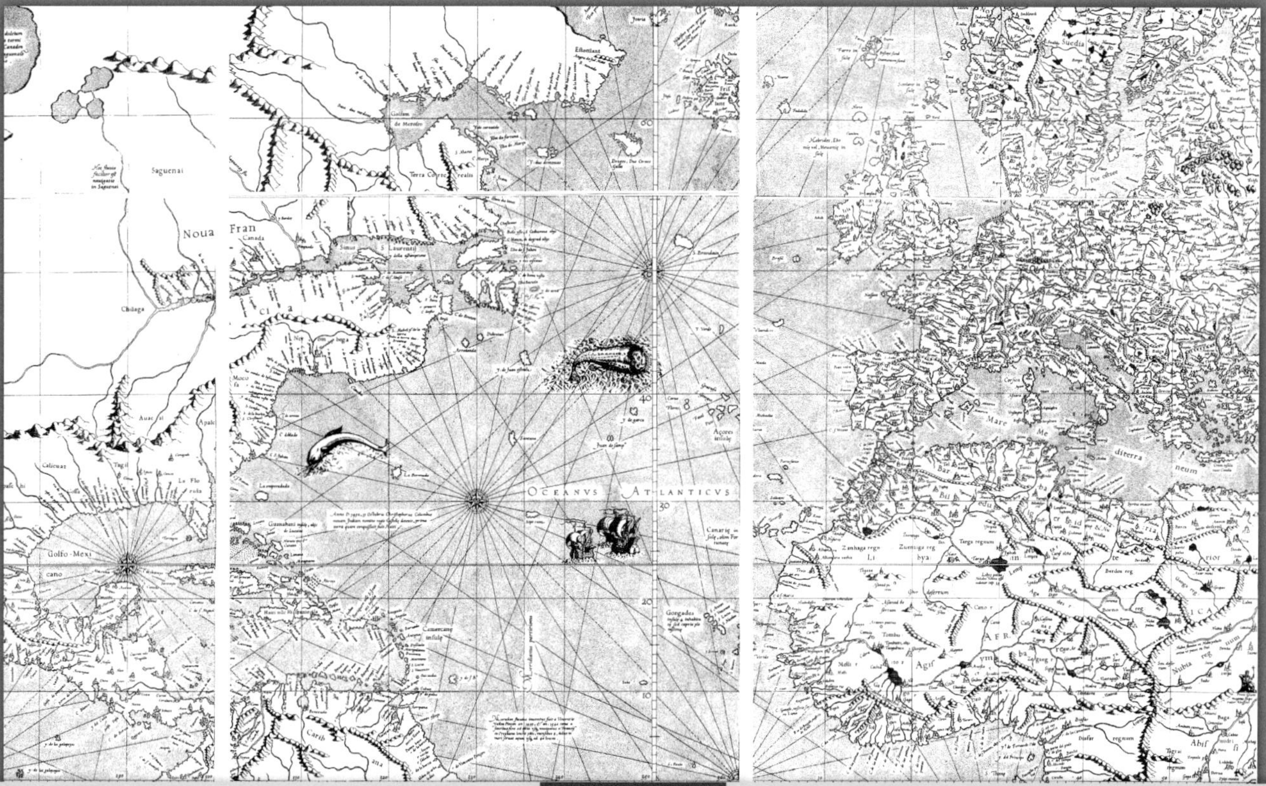

1569

Flemish geographer Gerardus Mercator (1512-1594) created a detailed world map. He designed a new way of showing the round Earth on a flat sheet of paper. On the map, Mercator stretched the size of the areas near the North and South poles. Though still not completely true to size, Mercator's map was more accurate than ancient maps.

Chapter 5

The Mathematics Revolution

1600—Mid-1700's

In the 1600's, scientists started to use mathematical ideas and **equations** when studying scientific topics. They collected data, tested theories in experiments, and explored new ideas, all using mathematics. Some scientists used mathematics to study *physics* (the study of matter and energy) and astronomy. In the early 1600's, Italian scientist Galileo Galilei experimented with weights and *pendulums* (weights swinging on a rod or rope). He invented mathematical laws to explain his scientific findings.

1609

German mathematician and astronomer Johannes Kepler (1571-1630) calculated the orbits of planets around the sun. Kepler's work proved Copernican theory.

1610

Italian scientist Galileo Galilei's (1564-1642) laws of pendulums and freely falling bodies helped found the science of mechanics, the study of forces and motion.

1614

Scottish mathematician John Napier (1550-1617) published the first table of *logarithms* (numbers known in algebra as *exponents*).

1637

French mathematician Pierre de Fermat (1601-1665) scribbled in the margin of a book that there is no whole number solution of the equation $xn + yn = zn$ if *n* is greater than 2. He noted he had a proof of this statement, but it was so long there was no room to write it down. "Fermat's last theorem" remained a challenge to mathematicians for 350 years, until British mathematician Andrew Wiles (1953-) finally published a proof in 1995.

In 1637, French philosopher and mathematician René Descartes (1596-1650) invented *analytic geometry* (using **algebra** to solve problems in **geometry**). He showed how lines on a graph can represent algebra equations. Descartes and fellow French mathematician Pierre de Fermat created **number theory.** Fermat's work laid the foundation for the branch of mathematics called **calculus.** In 1654, Fermat and Blaise Pascal puzzled over the chances of winning at card or dice games. After this conversation, Pascal invented a triangle to calculate probable wins and losses. In "Pascal's triangle," each number in any row is the sum of the two numbers directly above it. This triangle was the beginning of a theory of **probability.**

French mathematician Blaise Pascal (1623-1662) invented a calculating machine. It had interlocking wheels and could add and subtract. This was an early version of a calculator. In the 1670's, Gottfried Wilhelm Leibniz (1646-1716) of Germany improved Pascal's calculator so that it could also multiply and divide.

1642

Fermat and Pascal explored probability theory, the foundation of modern *statistics* (methods used to gather and analyze information).

1654

The Mathematics Revolution

1600—Mid-1700's

In the mid-1600's, English scientist, astronomer, and mathematician Sir Isaac Newton changed people's view of the universe. From 1665 to 1667, Newton made historic discoveries about light, color, motion, and **gravitation.**

By passing a beam of sunlight through a glass **prism,** Newton showed that white light is made up of a rainbowlike band of colors. Newton's most important discovery was a universal force called *gravitation.* Newton realized that the same force that makes a pebble fall to the ground keeps the moon traveling around Earth and the planets traveling around the sun. He found that simple

1684 and 1686

Leibniz published his theories of **calculus** in two works, the first in 1684 and the second in 1686. Studying independently, Sir Isaac Newton (1642-1727) published his work on calculus in 1687.

Late 1600's

Gottfried Wilhelm Leibniz invented the **binary number system.** This system calculates with just two **digits:** 0 and 1. For centuries, no one could find a use for binary mathematics. But today, most computers are programmed using the binary system. Computer code is written in 1's and 0's.

mathematical **equations** could explain both falling pebbles and moving planets. Newton's three laws of motion explain how force and **mass** affect the movement of objects. These significant laws are still used in almost every branch of scientific study, especially engineering.

From the late 1600's into the 1700's, several generations of a Swiss family, the Bernoullis, made important contributions to the field of mathematics. Jakob Bernoulli (1654-1705) explored analytic **geometry** and **probability** theory. Jakob's brother, Johann (1667-1748), worked on analytic geometry, astronomy, and physics. One of Johann's sons, Daniel (1700-1782), used mathematics to study the motion of fluids and discovered a law of physics still used today called *Bernoulli's principle.*

Newton published his laws of motion and gravitation in his book known as *Principia mathematica (Mathematical Principles).*

1687

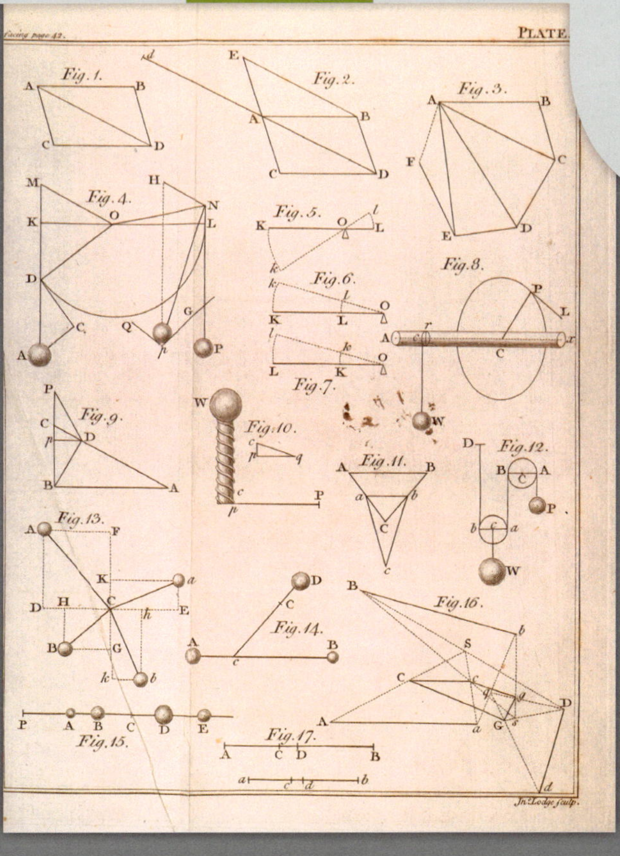

1735

English clockmaker John Harrison (1693-1776) invented the first accurate time-keeper for navigation at sea. It is called a *chronometer.* Most navigators used the positions of the sun and stars to find their way at sea. But to navigate this way, sailors needed to know the exact time. Harrison's chronometer allowed sailors to more accurately calculate their positions at sea.

Chapter 6

Mathematics and Machines

Late 1700's—Early 1930's

In the late 1700's and early 1800's, a period of rapid change called the *Industrial Revolution* took place in society. As steam-powered machines were used to produce goods in factories, inventors used mathematics to program these machines to work automatically—without human input.

In 1801, French weaver Joseph Marie Jacquard invented an automated *loom* (weaving machine). The Jacquard loom had cards with punched holes to control the threads. Different cards could be inserted to make different patterns of cloth,

1801

French weaver Joseph Marie Jacquard (1752-1834) invented a loom controlled by a punch-card system.

English mathematician Charles Babbage (1791-1871) designed his analytical engine. Although the machine was never fully built in his lifetime, this device was the most advanced "computing machine" designed at the time. Later, inventors built his designs.

1830's

following "hole" or "no hole" commands. This method is similar to calculating using only two **digits,** 0 and 1, as in **binary** mathematics.

In the 1820's, English mathematician Charles Babbage designed a computing machine, called the *difference engine.* In the 1830's he designed a more complex *analytical engine.* Although Babbage never built his designs, his work predicted important ideas of modern computing, including the idea of "memory."

In the mid-1800's British mathematician George Boole (1815-1864) created a new "**algebra** of **logic**," or *Boolean algebra*. His system could represent logical ideas as mathematical symbols. For example, the number 1 could represent "true" and 0 could represent "false." Modern computers rely on such a system.

1843

Ada Lovelace (1815-1852), English mathematician and daughter of the poet Lord Byron (1788-1824), published *Sketch of the Analytical Engine.* This paper described how Babbage's analytical engine could perform different tasks. She pioneered the idea that different **programs** could run on the same machine or computer.

1864

Scottish scientist and mathematician James Clerk Maxwell (1831-1879) showed how light, magnetism, and electricity are related. He combined the laws of magnetism and electricity into four important **equations.**

1870's

German mathematician Georg Cantor (1845-1918) developed **set theory,** the logical foundation of mathematics. He was the first to explore the mathematics of *infinity* (an amount that has no limit).

Mathematics and Machines

Late 1700's—Early 1930's

The first computing machines had little practical use. Charles Babbage's machine was so impractical that he never built it. In the late 1800's, however, people began putting computing machines to work.

In 1888, American computer pioneer Hermann Hollerith invented an electric calculating machine. It used punch cards to handle huge amounts of data, including the returns from the U.S. Census of 1890. In one day, 56 Hollerith "tabulating" machines worked through the census details of more than 6 million people. Before Hollerith's invention, human workers counted such details by hand.

American inventor Herman Hollerith's (1860-1929) tabulating machines processed large amounts of information from the U.S. Census of 1890.

1890

1894

French mathematician and physicist Henri Poincaré (1854-1912) published the first paper about topology. In topology, a figure's precise shape does not matter. Instead, topology studies the unique properties of the shapes. Poincaré's many contributions to mathematics laid the groundwork for German-born physicist Albert Einstein's theories of relativity.

Meanwhile, mathematics continued to help scientists and inventors. German-born *physicist* (a scientist who studies matter and energy) Albert Einstein changed the way people thought about time, space, motion, and gravity. He developed new ideas in mathematics and **geometry**—such as the idea that space can be curved. In Einstein's *special theory of relativity,* he introduced a now famous **equation:** $E = mc^2$. This equation means a body's energy (E) equals the body's **mass** (m) times the speed of light squared ($c \times c$). The speed of light (c) is 186,282 miles (299,792 kilometers) per second!

1905

Albert Einstein (1879-1955) excited the scientific world with his *special theory of relativity.* He showed the mathematical relationships between **mass** and energy, and between space and time. In 1915, Einstein published another work, this one on the *general theory of relativity.* In this work, Einstein shows how mass causes space to curve.

1910-1913

British philosophers Alfred North Whitehead (1861-1947) and Bertrand Russell (1872-1970) described a logical foundation for mathematics in the three-volume book called *Principia Mathematica*. They believed all mathematics to be based on **logic.**

1931

Austrian-born American mathematician Kurt Gödel (1906-1978) showed that mathematics cannot be complete. He found that there will always be mathematical or logical statements that can be neither proved nor disproved. Gödel's theorem influenced the development of modern computers.

Chapter 7

Early Electronic Computers

Mid-1930's—Early 1970's

What is a computer? In the simplest sense, a computer is a machine that performs mathematics. In the early 1900's, many computing machines appeared in factories and offices. But these machines could only perform one task. In 1936, a new idea of computing was on the horizon. British mathematician Alan Turing proposed the idea of a "universal computing machine" that could run several **programs** used for different tasks. Today's computers are based on this idea. A modern computer can run many different kinds of programs, or instructions, at the same time.

1936

British mathematician Alan Turing (1912-1954) proposed a "universal computing machine." This computer could rewrite its own instructions. It could even run instructions copied from other computers. Turing's machine was just an idea, not a real device. But computers today work in a similar way. A smartphone, for example, can download many programs called *apps.* The apps carry instructions for the computer to follow.

1936

The first Fields Medal was awarded to two mathematicians: Lars Valerian Ahlfors (1907-1996) of Finland and Jesse Douglas (1897-1965) of the United States. The Fields Medal is often called the Nobel Prize of mathematics.

1939

German inventor Konrad Zuse (1910-1995) designed an electronic computer. It could run different programs for different engineering tasks. This type of computer could run at electronic speeds without manual reprogramming slowing down its process.

World War II (1939-1945) led to rapid progress in computer science. Germany used **cryptography,** especially the Enigma code, to send secret messages. The United States and Great Britain, among the nations fighting against Germany and its allies, developed powerful electronic computers to help break these codes. British engineer Tommy Flowers led a team that built an advanced codebreaking computer called the Colossus.

After the war ended, a huge electronic computer called the Electronic Numerical Integrator and Computer (ENIAC) began operation. ENIAC could be reprogrammed. Computer specialists created different programs by setting switches manually and plugging cables into the machine's panels. ENIAC helped pave the way for realizing Turing's vision: Computers that could run many programs for many tasks.

1944

British engineer Tommy Flowers (1905-1998) led a team that developed the Colossus computer for decoding the Enigma code. Colossus helped lead to Germany's defeat during World War II.

1946

One of the first programmable electronic computers, ENIAC, started operation. Two engineers at the University of Pennsylvania, J. Presper Eckert, Jr. (1919-1995) and John William Mauchly (1907-1980), built the machine. ENIAC was enormous! It had 17,500 **vacuum tubes**—bulky devices that carry electronic signals. Those signals stand for numbers. ENIAC took up about as much floor space as an average single family house.

Early Electronic Computers

Mid-1930's—Early 1970's

Computers of the 1940's were massive, expensive machines. They were often kept in huge rooms in secure buildings. Today, even more powerful computers, such as tablets and smartphones, fit in our hands. No other technology has become so small and powerful as quickly as the computer. This trend towards technology becoming smaller and smaller began with a device called a **transistor.**

In 1947, three American scientists, John Bardeen (1908-1991), Walter H. Brattain (1902-1987), and William Shockley (1910-1989), invented the transistor. Transistors are tiny electronic switches. They can represent the number 1 by

1947

The transistor, a tiny electronic switch, was invented. Transistors are placed on computer chips which hold computer **programs** and data. These small chips soon replaced bulky vacuum tubes in computers.

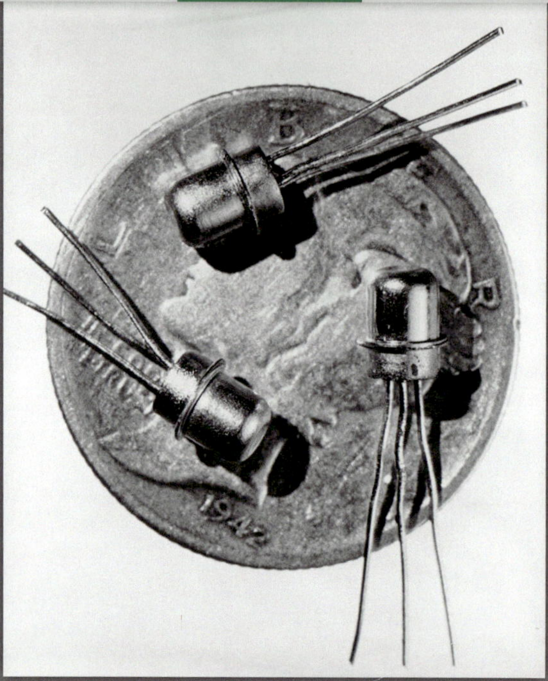

1951

The American-built Electronic Discrete Variable Automatic Computer (EDVAC) was the first computer with a **central processing unit** (**CPU**). The CPU acts like a computer's "brain." Hungarian-American mathematician John von Neumann (1903-1957) developed the idea of a CPU. Almost all computers today are based on his work.

1958

American engineer Seymour Cray (1925-1996) designed the first all-transistor computer.

1958

Jack Kilby (1923-2005), an American engineer, invented the integrated circuit. Circuits allow computers to function. Kilby's device fit a tiny circuit with transistors onto the surface of a single silicon chip. Kirby shared credit for this device with American physicist Robert Noyce (1927-1990), who also invented an integrated circuit while working on his own.

switching "on," or represent the number 0 by switching "off." The **numerals** 1 and 0 work as **binary digits,** called *bits.* By stringing 1's and 0's together, the numbers can form a code for any type of information. Today, people write code for all of the programs that run on a computer. Earlier computers used bulky **vacuum tubes** to stand for information. Transistors are smaller and faster than vacuum tubes.

Computer engineers continued to shrink transistors. More of the transistors could fit onto computer chips, or small cards that hold data. Almost all computers perform their calculations on chips made of silicon, a material with special electrical properties. The more transistors that could fit on a chip, the more effective a computer could be. During the 1960's, computers built with these chips became both small and powerful enough that they could be sent on space flights.

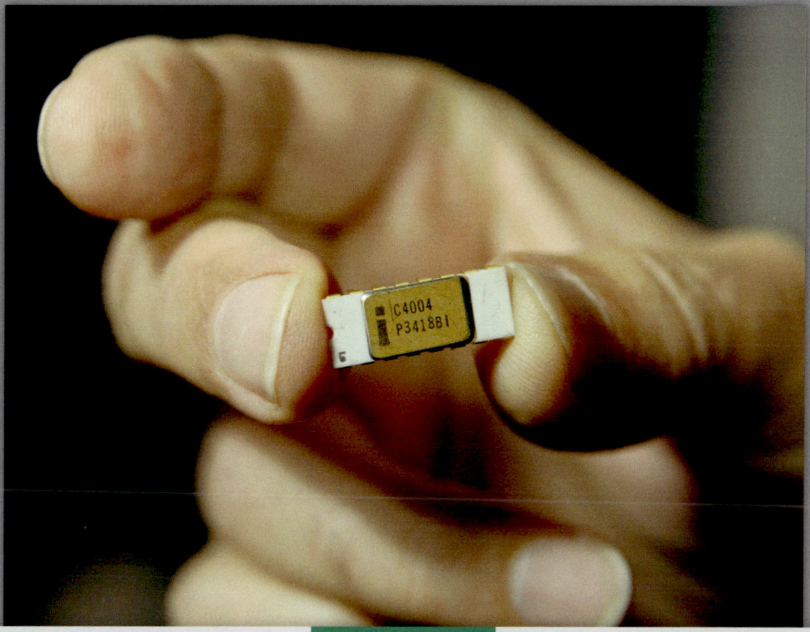

Late 1960's

The United States military developed ARPAnet. This network linked together computer systems across the country. ARPAnet laid the foundation for the Internet.

1967

A team at the American company Texas Instruments, Inc. invented the first working handheld calculator.

1971

Intel Corporation, founded by Gordon Moore, (1929-   ) developed the first microprocessor. A microprocessor is a CPU located on a single chip. Moore predicted that computer chips would double in power about every two years. His prediction, called "Moore's law," proved correct for the next 40 years. The first microprocessor built in 1971 had 2,500 transistors. Modern chips are the same size but have billions of transistors.

Chapter 8

Computers Everywhere

Mid-1970's—Today

In the early 1970's, most computers were used in businesses and government operations. They were too bulky and complicated for people to use at home. In 1975, the first small home computer, the Altair, went on sale to the public. The computer was sold as a kit for people to assemble, or build, at home. Two Americans named Bill Gates and Paul Allen founded a company called Microsoft Corporation. They use advanced mathematical concepts to write computer **programs** for the Altair.

1975

The first personal computer, the Altair, was released.

Apple Computer, Inc. (now Apple Inc.) was founded by Americans Steve Jobs (1955-2011) and Steve Wozniak (1950-). The Apple II personal computer, released the following year, cost less than the big, powerful computers used by businesses. The Apple II computer was sold as an assembled unit, so people did not need to be experts to build or use it.

American inventors Bill Gates (1955-) and Paul Allen (1953-) founded Microsoft Corporation.

1975

1976

Americans Steven Jobs and Stephen Wozniak founded Apple Computer, Inc. in 1976. They sold a home computer that needed no assembly. In 1981, International Business Machines Corporation (IBM) offered its first personal computer (PC) to the public. Soon, small computers became common in homes, schools, and offices.

By the early 1990's, some computers were connected to the Internet. But the Internet's main users were computer scientists and military staff. In 1991, British scientist Tim Berners-Lee developed the World Wide Web. The Web made it easy to use the Internet from a personal computer. Soon, the amount of information available on the Web greatly increased. Companies developed computer programs called *search engines.* The search engines helped people enter a keyword to more easily find information online.

1991

British scientist Tim Berners-Lee (1955-) introduced the World Wide Web. Berners-Lee was working at the European Organization for Nuclear Research (CERN) near Geneva, Switzerland, when he had the idea for the World Wide Web. He thought the Web would help other scientists link to CERN's computer files. Today, people can use the Web to search for information about almost anything.

1998

Google, Inc. launched its search engine. It helped people find information on the vast World Wide Web. Google's search engine works by counting links to websites. If many links lead to a given website, the search engine gives the website a higher rank, or level, in the results.

2002

The BlackBerry® was the first popular smartphone, a phone that works like a small computer. A modern smartphone has more computing power than the NASA computers used on the Apollo moon-landing mission in 1969.

Computers Everywhere

Mid-1970's—Today

Since the early 2000's, mobile-computer use has skyrocketed, becoming commonplace in many areas of the world. Such mobile devices as laptops, cell phones, and tablets are designed to be small and portable. They often wirelessly connect to the Internet. Advanced cell phones are called *smartphones.* Smartphones work like small computers. The user downloads programs called *apps* to the phone. In 2010, Apple released the iPad®, a tablet computer about the size of a magazine. Like the iPhone®, the iPad had a touch screen and could display websites and run more complicated computer **programs.** Through computers and mobile devices, the Internet changed the way people communicate.

2007

The Apple iPhone was the first widely used smartphone with touch-screen controls. Such controls are now common on many computers, including tablets.

2011

Another developing branch of computer science is *artificial intelligence* (AI)—a computer's ability to copy intelligent human behavior. In 2011, IBM developed an AI computer called Watson. It demonstrated an advanced ability to understand the human language. Watson beat two human champions on "Jeopardy!," a challenging question-and-answer television quiz show.

The Internet made it easier for people to connect with one another on a daily basis—all by using computer technology.

Some companies and governments run huge data centers. A data center may contain tens of thousands of computers. The computers might store and process the data for popular websites. Or, they may work together to solve scientific problems. Mathematical advances have affected nearly every aspect of daily life. Computers have become so powerful that they can listen and speak to people, drive cars, and even send spacecraft to other planets. Despite such advances, researchers face many challenges in their attempts to make ever-smaller, more powerful computers. But if history is any guide, the next great discovery in mathematics and computer science could completely change the world—again.

Iranian mathematician Maryam Mirzakhani (1977-) won a Fields Medal for her work studying abstract mathematical spaces. She used computer programs to help perform her work. Mirzakhani is the first woman to win this important top prize in mathematics.

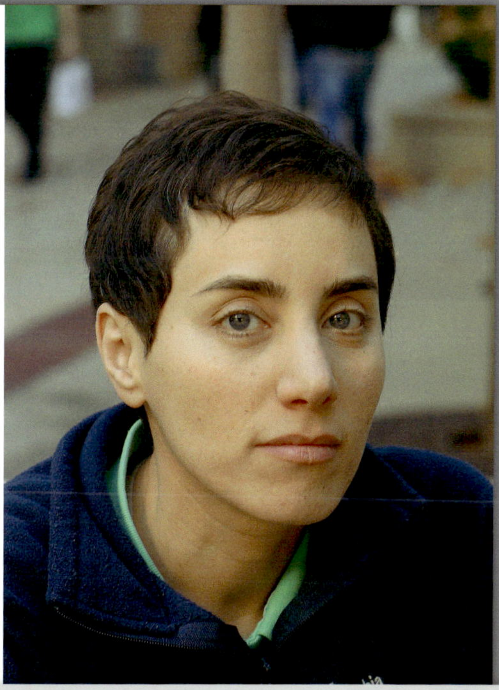

2012

Researchers created a **transistor** out of a single atom. The experimental device showed the limits of Moore's law—transistors cannot shrink below the size of an atom. At sizes smaller than atoms, the laws of electronics break down.

2014

2016

Researchers used computers to find the largest known prime number yet. It would take dozens of pages to write it out fully, but it can be written as a formula:

$$2^{74,207,281} - 1.$$

Glossary

algebra a branch of mathematics that uses letters to stand for unknown amounts.

binary number system a numbering system that uses two digits—1 and 0. The system groups numbers by twos and powers of two. **Binary** means "two at a time."

calculus an advanced branch of mathematics that deals with changing quantities.

CPU (central processing unit) the "brain" of a computer where information is processed.

cryptography the study of secret writing systems that use codes and ciphers.

digit a single numeral used to represent numbers. The numerals 0, 1, 2, 3, 4, 5, 6, 7, 8, and 9 are digits.

equation a statement in mathematics of equality between two quantities, indicated by the equal sign (=) between them.

geometry a branch of mathematics that studies the shape, size, and position of lines, angles, curves, and figures.

gravitation the force of attraction between all objects because of their mass.

logic the art of reasoning.

mass the amount of matter in an object.

Middle Ages the period in European history between ancient and modern times, from about the A.D. 400's through about the 1400's. The end date depends on the region of Europe considered.

number theory a branch of mathematics that deals with *integers* (whole numbers and their negatives) and a type of whole number called prime numbers.

numeral a written symbol for a number.

pi the ratio of the *circumference* (outer boundary line) of a circle to its *diameter* (line that crosses a circle at its center). It is almost equal to 3.14159, but pi cannot be written exactly. It is also represented with the symbol π.

prime number a whole number greater than 1 that can only be divided evenly by itself and by 1. For example, 2, 3, 5, and 7 are prime, but 4 and 6 are not.

prism a solid with two parallel bases joined by three or more sides.

probability a branch of mathematics that tries to express how likely an event is to happen.

program(s) instructions for a computer.

Renaissance a great cultural movement that began in Italy during the early 1300's.

set theory a branch of mathematics and logic that groups ideas together into collections, called sets.

square angle a type of angle that always measures 90 degrees. Also called a right angle.

transistor a tiny device that controls the flow of electricity in computers and other electronic devices.

trigonometry a branch of mathematics that studies the relationships between the sides and angles of triangles.

vacuum tube a sealed glass tube from which almost all of the air has been removed.

Find Out More

Books

Ada Byron Lovelace and the Thinking Machine by Laurie Wallmark (Creston Books, 2015)

Computer by Mike Goldsmith (DK Publishing, 2011)

The Greatest Mathematician: Archimedes and His Eureka! Moment by Paul Hightower (Enslow Publishers, 2010)

We've Got Your Number by Mukul Patel (Kingfisher, 2013)

Who Is Bill Gates? by Patricia Brennan Demuth (Grosset & Dunlap, 2013)

Why Pi? by Johnny Ball (DK Publishing, 2009)

Websites

Computer History Museum – The Babbage Engine
http://www.computerhistory.org/babbage/
Take an in-depth look at the first automatic computing engine designed by English computer pioneer Charles Babbage.

Computer History Museum – Timeline of Computer History
http://www.computerhistory.org/timeline/
Interact with a photo timeline of important events in the history of computing, from the 1930's to the present.

National Geographic Kids – Absolute Genius
http://kids.nationalgeographic.com/explore/absolute-genius/
Watch an entertaining explanation of the genius of the ancient Greek mathematician Archimedes.

National Geographic Kids – Mapping
http://education.nationalgeographic.org/mapping/
Test your map skills, play mapping games, and create your own map of the world.

Nova – The Great Math Mystery
http://www.pbs.org/wgbh/nova/physics/great-math-mystery.html
Learn how past and present peoples explored the mysteries of mathematics by watching a short video.

PBS LearningMedia – Base 60: Babylonian Decimals
http://www.pbslearningmedia.org/resource/mgbh.math.nbt.babylon/base-60-babylonian-decimals/
Learn about the base 60 number system of the ancient Babylonians with a video, activity, and handout aligned with the U.S. Common Core State Standards.

Index